ORANGE-ROSE AND SHADOW

New Women's Voices Series, No. 166

poems by

JEANNIE GAMBILL

Finishing Line Press
Georgetown, Kentucky

ORANGE-ROSE AND SHADOW

For our mother
Mary Matilda Roberts Black
in tribute to her twenty-year tenacious
struggle with Alzheimer's Disease

ACKNOWLEDGMENTS

I gratefully acknowledge the editors of the following journals in which these poems
first appeared:

Plainsongs (Hastings, Nebraska): "Pour Water on Me"
Voices de la Luna (San Antonio, Texas): "Light Bending"

Sincere thanks to Finishing Line Press for selecting *Orange-Rose and Shadow*
for publication in their New Women's Voices Series, and especially to my editor,
Christen Kincaid, for shepherding the book's production.

Thanks to Robin Reagler for her deliberate and warm guidance during this book's
preparation, to Kathleen Cook and Loueva Smith for their careful reading and
feedback, and to Carolyn Dahl for her professional guidance.

I'm grateful to the dedicated members of my long-running poetry group, including
Eric Avera, Margo Davis, Kathleen Cook, Stan Crawford, Priscilla Frake, Lewis
Garvin, Carol Munn, Sally Ridgeway, and Rebecca Spears, for the commitment we
share and for their specific feedback on the early drafts of these poems.

I owe more than I can express to Sasha West for her steadfast encouragement, her
inspiring, broadening critique of my poems, and her generous, imaginative teaching.

To Clint, my husband, and our family, I rely on your continuous loving support

Publisher: Leah Huete de Maines
Editor: Christen Kincaid
Cover Art: Johnathan Roberts
Author Photo: Harley Gambill
Cover Design: Elizabeth Maines McCleavy

Order online: www.finishinglinepress.com
also available on amazon.com

Author inquiries and mail orders:
Finishing Line Press
PO Box 1626
Georgetown, Kentucky 40324
USA

Table of Contents

Orange-Rose and Shadow

Back home, the Deep South, she was eager
to get to the pond before dark, the walk
on silk-sandy lanes, pole in hand.
Purpled bullaces, barely visible, hung
on large-leafed vines that intertwined
a wire fence and settled upward into the trees.
The other side of the fence, another grassier
lane and then corn. The pecan trees
near the fence, shadowing one—
or the other—lane.

> In West Texas, her home after marriage,
> this earth-dug tank where she fished,
> there's time to study sockets
> left by cow's hooves in dried flesh-colored
> clay at the water's edge and in mud
> just under the water's surface.

Georgia or Texas, she did not
use a net to take up fish that dangled
or thrashed at the end of her line.
With her hand, she grasped the fish—
avoiding fins—worked the mouth free of the hook,
strung the fish through its gill and then mouth
onto an anchored line that allowed the fish the water.
And with a worm or minnow
baited her hook, dropped her line again
until the red-and-white floater
was buoyed. The floater had to be watched,
seeing too, then—in her two
worlds—the evening light . . .

In Georgia, this horizontal slant
glossing the pond's dark
swamp waters. Cypress, tall
or knuckled near the surface,
still and faintly mirrored.

Or in West Texas,
an orange-rose dusk that agitates
the banked side of the tank, its scattering
of rocks. And the other side,
where mesquites and scrub oak
assume both orange-rose and shadow.

And I, offspring of her two worlds,
not seeing until now how she *was* there.
I—so afraid that these waters
these branches   the shadings   this
sand   these rocks—
this milk of my endurance
my breath   my keeping—
so afraid—from young to now—
that I might not
be returned enough to its wellspring.
So *of myself* there, that I could not see
my need in her, could not see
her exchanges.

She, now moved through
to another light.
I will seed myself

where the wild sweet bitter-skinned grapes
hide, visible only when eyes
laze over what there is to see,
when the breath slows with step and step
to the long exhale of a dark
glaze, the pond's surface,
and lifts, as these cypress
from tea-colored waters

and where some unencumbered
un-treed sky spills
its late-day light onto banked earth
and sunken cow prints, stilling
the heat, reviving
the grasshopper's chirp and buzz.

You, Whole Again

You come through the back door
of my house. As you walk, a stream
of words in whole sentences
spills from your mouth,
and you call me, *Jeannie*.
You wear a dress of polished cotton,
distinct grey and white, a wide belt
the same fabric as the dress.

I watch you walk free of weakness,
free of adult diapers,

and I listen—your voice, un-caged,
given back.

This full-skirted dress, its crisp sounds,
your brisk steps—like your walk
and the dresses you wore
when all of your children
were of your house.

We sit. I, in the rocking chair
across from you on the sofa.
You talk of the others—
my brothers, my sister,
news from your Sis back home.
Then you tell me about one side
of you that isn't working
just right,

and I follow
your optimistic
flow of talk.

What Will Remain

This journey home, congregants accompany me
en route: these weathered grasses,

straw-colored, their seed pods frothy,
and grasses still slightly blue hued;

and broom weed's yellow-topped blooms
that dust field after field; and, near Brenham,

the earth's beginning its subtle rise and fall,
slopes of tended lawns. The Callahan Divide,

closer home, mounding the earth, curvatures
lined against the sky like written word

scribed in me, read and reread. Then the one
solitary hill, a sentinel advancing

the last stretch where an eruption of plateaus
crowd the road and then fall away as arms

opening—a clarion gesture
announcing the basin,

the town.   Stunned with adrenalin's
ache, I wonder what will remain

of her and her keeper.

~~~

She is holding onto
a ladder while he reaches into the pecan tree.

She and I sit in the swing. She, not knowing—
as you and I think of knowing—that I ever

left. Now animated, she chatters, her speech
skewed, a fanciful grounding

in her physical self. She points to swollen
knuckles, tries to bend the fourth finger—

stiff and unyielding—a playful grimace
on her face like I as a child acted out

for her some discernable grief. Then she strokes
white long splotches on each finger,

white-white, obvious against garden-browned
skin. Disjointed phrases tumble out

while we examine her hands and she pets
my arm. My *double-minded stuff,* she names

the white splotches. Sputters of broken language,
spirit-talk, leaking this earth bound vessel.

Then Visit Me With Willows

My mother balls up her clothes,
puts them in a paper sack, and my father
must drive her into the country,
or take her to a friend's house where they sing
or play dominoes, until she is pulled back
and is no longer frantic
to get to her mother, long dead.

Late in life, it seems one's mother
often returns. As with my mother
and a close friend, these women, caught
in un-turned time, their mothers now present
again, and they speak of her often, or gesture
work tasks beside her, or determine

a way to her. My mother now
belt-cinches her clothes as though
her waist held tight—and always
the one particular hat—could carry her
home, could hold her, could help her
navigate her mind's turns.

Alone, after a visit home, I turn
onto the highway, the music loud—
Jericho Road—and I, with it,
singing. I assume this route,
its surroundings, the changing terrain
this often traveled road. The creeks' slopes

here clothed in willows and the willows
arrayed in subtle maroon-red hues. This turn
out of late winter—this baring of color—
a surprise. These willows' branches, not snarled

as the scrub oaks', nor from the tree's trunk
twisting outward. Rather, each limb lifting
from a grounded center, the willows'
tinged limbs earth-anchored
then lifting up, up.   My Houston home,

a long drive, I turn the radio off, clothed
in these willows, their red-hued gestures,
and spirited among them, a chorus of obstinate
women, arms upstretched, searching home.

Where They Will Take Care of You

You will not want to hear of this—
                                    our moving you
from home   to the room
where they will take care of you.
                    Can you hear us? Your language, now
shattered. Your knowing or not knowing,
a literal unknown to us.

                    All difficult
discernment, what had been *decided*
as the way we must go—now obscured
the moment we get the call, the nursing home—

A place has become available for her.

                            We try to move
ourselves through what must be done,
stirring your things to choose something
for you to take with you.
                            The hallowed
clock that you stare at—your mother's—
cannot go. Your room, not private
enough for its ticking, its chime.
                            And your clothes,
your large-billed orange hat, the stained
shirt, its long sleeves that you wear buttoned,
turned-up secure near the elbows, and
the pink cotton pants, the black frayed
leather belt—these clothes you require,
as though each morning seizing
some semblance of yourself.

                    How can we send you
with these worn stained clothes?
                    How send this morning sun,
its slant through floor-length windows, the porch room
where you now bed?
                    How transport the sounds
of this house—your dear one's constant whistling
and his whistling and movements in the garden
just outside the window?

I watch the teapot, wait for the water's
stir, wait for a blossoming, these leaves.

All That You Tended

The ratio of self
to home: one part
in seventy.
    Kay Ryan

I would enter your house,
and before finding you, idle
in the noise that peals

from these furnishings. Your mother's
clock on the mantel, its pendulum
unmoving, its chime unprovoked,

yet its sound unburied, its sonorous
clamor startling the room. The studio piano
where sister sister brother practiced and you,

there, playing hymns, your touch bouncy,
staccato-like, your fingernails
click-a-click on the keys. The low coffee table,

its drawers, a mess of playing cards
and trinkets—the grandchildren's
plunder. And in the kitchen

this recipe box you decoupaged—
lift the lid. Your handwriting,
ornamental, scrolled across index cards

and folded into paper.
This kitchen, your tools—minimal,
utilitarian, worn as the one cutting board,

the wood darkened, a smooth
scented sheen from years of use.
And behind glass-paned

doors, this built-in hutch—your artistic
uncluttered arrangement of pottery,
the blue and grey-white pitcher,

salt-glazed, as this brown pitcher
of Aunt Madge's, and from my sister's wheel,
a bowl perfected in burnt orange,

and odd pieces, cut-glass or painted
porcelain.　　　　　This porch room,
the ferns you water,

and the Christmas cactus, its output
faithful in red blooms.
　　　　　　　　　The house's

belongings breathe and utter—resound
some settled and undistracted
greeting.

　　　　　　　　　While here,
this place you now home, metal-framed
glass double doors grate as I gain

entrance. Then just inside, an obligatory
conscious retrieval of names,
and then greetings, these nurses

and aides at their station. The hallway,
a negotiation of wheel chairs, my palm
on a drooped shoulder,

and another. I do not fully
admit these necessary acts,
this broaching of so many layers,

this long approach to you
in your room, asleep in your chair.
I kiss you awake

and push your chair past
the dining room to a well-appointed
foyer and seating area where

we wait at a small table
for your meal tray. My hand
along your upper back or shoulder

while your hands pantomime actions—
snapping beans or shelling peas—some part of you
inhabiting another time, another place.

          There is so little here
to help.   This place,
these surroundings, not

of you.   Yet, you and I—
and the others who come to you—
         trying to bear   what was promised

when your un-naming had begun
and you knew, and could speak
your fear, and I could promise

We will not let you forget
who you are.

Before the Orange Large-Billed Hat?

Did you know her when she sat on the sofa at day's end,
one knee elevated, with the heel of her bare foot on the cushion's
edge or across the other knee, the newspaper spread in front of her
as she read the paper and peeled and ate an orange?

Did you know her when she dressed herself—stylishly? Dresses,
with pleated or slightly gathered skirt, polished cotton, or a satin
finish that sashayed when she walked. Or knit ensembles,
and patent shoes, some kind of flair about the shoes—understated,
but not plain. And stockings, even in the West Texas scorch
of summer, or the moisture-hung heat, South Georgia.

Were you able to notice her when she carried out her plans,
determined and with little fanfare? The dumpling's dough, rolled-out,
cut to squares, transported between sheets of wax paper to the cabin
at the lake, cooked there with chicken and broth. The cabin's beds
fresh with clean linens. The cabin swept and mopped.

Did you ever see her when she took quick naps, her arm
along the sofa's back, her head resting there? She, the last
to repose, the first to tend you, dress you, re-dress you, then watch
as you kicked water, the small pool. The first to organize fishing
tackle, help with your shoes, your jacket, the life-jacket,
bait the hook, support the pole—your hand, too,
on the pole with hers. She, all the while, improvising fishing songs,
bathing songs, dressing songs—*this* little sock on *this* little foot,
this *dear* little foot . . .

Did you ever hear her erupt into the conversation? Her reticent
demeanor ruffled—some defense, some argument she couldn't stifle.
Her presence in the circle awakened?

                              What did you know of her before
the orange large-billed hat she wouldn't be without, before the pants
she insisted on, a tight draw at the waist, the one belt she could

manage? What did you know before he had to coax her to bathe?
And often, of necessity, drove with her into the country to calm
her obstinate resolve to go home—and she was home—when she
had rolled up her clothes, put them in her purse, distraught to leave,
to get to her mother, who was no longer living?

I know you knew her—had taken to her—each book she read to you,
your extended summer visits, and the summer, book by book,
she potty-trained you, and when she played with you in the striped
tent that she had sewn and easily set up, a folding table draped
in red and white, you and she trailing the other in and out,
until worn out.

I know you know her. Though now, I can't re-figure, in the decades-
long schedule of loss, where and how, along the trajectories—
your gaining in what you were able to know, while herself's
slow un-naming—and I, so displaced, each small abandonment,
not noticing—in ways as to remember—how exactly
you might have known her . . . until now . . . lately . . .

                                                    I've wondered

if you knew her when—though in a rush to go—she'd steal a moment
at her dressing table, tilt the near-empty bottle of crimson nail polish,
dig to find lacquer . . .

                    did you know her when, still, she polished her nails?

Pour Water on Me

She was at one of the windows,
in a wheel chair—this woman
I didn't know—her face
right up to the window,
almost touching.
Heavy maroon drapes
framed each window—
framed her—
framed the enactment.
Her focus
just outside the window
into a courtyard.

Her utterances
were like weeping,
and she did weep
quietly
and she spoke,
You are so beautiful.
Why don't you come in.
Please come in
and pour
water on me.

I heard it
as I passed behind her
on the way to find
my mother.
The woman at the window,
a constant stream of moaning
and whimpers
asking the one
outside—
where there was no one—
to come in
to her.

My mother
speaks rarely
and in broken bits.
She performs
actions—
shelling peas, I think,
and putting something
pot to pot. Often
she works the seams
of my clothes
like she was fitting
a dress to me,
the dress wrong-side-out,
and she had pinned
the seams
where she would sew.
Now tugging at my clothes,
arguing with what I wore that day,
wanting the shoulder seams
to rest
in a different place.

One day
my mother
was pouring
something.
She lifted
the unseen
vessel—
tilting it,
pouring.
I wanted to catch the liquid
in my hands,

bend over
put my head
under the spout,
feel
this stream
she drained
from her
pitcher.
I wanted it to flow
over me,
what she poured
into the air
invisible
as the scrim
its loose folds
encircling us.

Light Bending

When I find myself again
among these purple-hued fields, I will have forgotten
that these fields collect light, dusk's quickening
that pronounces the grasses, close-

cropped where cows eat, and the taller grasses,
each blade, a luminary, and the wire fence
and fence posts, and these scrub oaks, scattered,
their branches' sturdy snarls. I'll have forgotten

that this tinged field light unfolds
the day. My father's hands, rotund fingers
cracked and stained from shelling pecans,
his touch rough as he cradles

my mother's head, her leaning to it
while she sips cranberry juice offered her. Forgotten
then his fidgeting, an incessant ruffling, a lozenge wrapper
or the edge of his calendar, while he talks,

while he listens.

            When I've come again
upon these fields, I'll wait,

                    complected
as this air   this grass   this day.

Last Rites

I was three
when my grandfather died.
My grandparent's living room
crowded with flowers
and his casket.
I dream
this living room
uncrowded,
work tables out,
two sewing machines.
Light from the windows
sufficient.
My sister, my mother,
my aunt, and I
sew burial clothes
for my grandmother.
Sometimes my mother isn't there,
and the requiem
we stitch and seam
is for her.
We work together
deciding
how the garments
will fit.

It was the two Marys
who went with oils
and cloth to prepare
the body of their friend.
The women,
in the sacred story,
who first saw him
alive after death.
Perhaps we fail this story,
when we immortalize the ending.

I want to return
to the ritual.
I want to be there
for the transition,
rub the spirit-house
with oil, swaddle
as at birth
the one returning.
When I must part
from one of mine,
let me have
a long farewell.
Sit with me,
and then,
let me be alone
with the body
and the flowers
in a house
where we've lived.

Present to Absence

I've seen it—the eyes, an absent
trough. One or another resident
at the nursing home, their wheelchair
parked in the hallway, a face
turned-up toward me—and in the eyes,
a chilling emptiness.

How to dwell in such absence?

                           Your gaze
was not vacant—ever. Day on day,
I'd work my way through a maze of hallways
and attendants and the roommate, a muddled
path to you. Years, your language broken,
your speech a jangle—though often
the inflection, the emotion, correct.
And then no utterances. But always you,
there, in your eyes.

                         As long as
*she wants to **be here**, as long as she knows*
where she is, I can't move her out of our home,
my father, saying. Almost a decade, you and he
navigating your decline—each day, each loss.
                    Then the stroke,
and it was clearly time.
                        Yet still, after the move, he with you
for extended visits, twice a day. Your face, a visible
shift, when the sound of his whistling
preceded him down the hall.

                          On a visit
back to your house, you approach
your mother's clock, the fireplace
mantel, and you stare and stare at it.

Your roommate, later, telling my sister
that you cried that night in your bed
in your room at the nursing home.

What could we do with this?

                    We paid attention
to the other signs—your sequenced
actions with your hands as though
you were somewhere else.

                    Were you more present
to absence than we could portion?

The ways I'd needed to see you
sifted from me now,
                    I sit before you, reread
your gracious holding on,
                              re-collect
what you bestowed—

all of those days
you returned my gaze.

Call Into the Shadows

So when [she] needed us most, we withdrew.
                Geraldine Brooks, *Sacred Chord*

Broken   The *we* of your jagged illness,
                twenty years, a progression of losses. The *you*,
                less and less *you*.

Not broken   We *were* there. We were
                not absent.

Broken   We straddled absence—evading
                what we could not face.

Broken   The expectations we—the husband, the daughters,
                the sons, the accumulating grandchildren—
                didn't know were there. Anticipating
                days with you as you.

Not broken   The laughter, you and I, when neither could recall
                why the oven was heating up. What else
                were we planning for supper?

Not broken   My finally asking . . . and your saying . . . *I'm afraid*
                I'll forget who I am.

Broken   A visit home, after weeks away, and I enter
                the house. You continue at the piano,
                an ordinary ease with me, talking to me
                while your hands still on the keys. No pause
                to greet me, no embrace, as though
                I had never left, as though I was not
                just returning.

Unbroken   A relentless accumulation of plaque, of protein
                that folds into your brain. Neurons disconnecting.
                A build-up of debris.

Not broken	*Brang! Brang!* Each hammer blow, my brother and I shattering the silence. Near midnight, the nursing home, and we are hanging photos the night before your arrival. This wall you would face in sleep each night and each daily nap for eleven years.
Broken	Your speech—nothing, eleven years.
Not broken	The husband's commitment—twice a day each day with you, feeding you lunch, feeding you dinner, waiting with you for the aide to help you to bed before the nap, before the night. Whistling. Patting. Kissing. Watching-over.
Not broken	Your face lifting when you heard his whistled song, his approach as he rounded the turn into the long hallway to you.
Not broken	Sitting near you at lunch, at dinner. He's fishing, and I'm in town, and you and I, at a small table, an open living room, removed from the others, from the noise. I lift the spoon, the fork to your mouth. I lean to you, my head against your head, and you lean to me.
Broken	The flood of sunlight, or the cold clear broad-skyed evening—each time one of us spills out into the un-confined. Leaving you inside. *I'll see you in a little while,* or, *I'll see you in the morning,* or, *I'll see you the next trip.* No language from you

to release us. The metal-rimmed glass door,
the abrasive sounds, its opening, its closing.
This deliverance into fatigued, energized,
guilty relief.

Still breaking   Your roommate's report about your crying
when we brought you back after a visit
home. That night, into the night, your face
turned to the wall, your long hard tears.

Still breaking   Where we put what was said—your crying
alone in the night. Even sister
to sister, not talking it out—putting it away.

Unbroken   Your solitary journey. When we turned to you,
when we turned away, when something in you
turned, clouded over, was taken from you,
and you knew, or you did not know. You,
ultimately alone
               each time   when   you turned,
and the one turning, and the one turned to
is the one alone—is you—is your own
self.

Still breaking, broken, breaking in   What did you know?
          Did you know?   more than we could hold?
more than we could have you know?
more than we now can hold—
what is broken   what is unbroken
what was   what is
still breaking?

Your Final Days

It's as though you're able to speak
again, your movements assertive—
an urging, a drive, perceptible
the weeks preceding your death.

               Hospice wisdom
avows that many of us, during our last days,
take charge—even though comatose,
or through hallucinations. We often
manage the final approach, wait
for someone to arrive, or for all to leave.

               Your body
sluffed from your bowels the dark
brackish announcement of your organs'
shutting down.

               Strange, this echo
of the infant's first elimination, the meconium,
its dark olive green, the infant's letting go
of all it had ingested in the womb.

               How we attend
every detail, the newly formed body—
all that is collected in the eyes,
or along the hairline, and in the distinctive
and variable first cries, and the one's
hands and feet—the unnamable

compilation of what is flesh and what is
spirit-breath—ourselves, attaching
to what is essentially no other
than this one.

And so, too, in the departing.

Summoned, your final hours, we gather
near your bed, your roommate curtained-off
and asleep. We take turns in the place
nearest your head—to whisper, to touch
your face with ours, a hand to rest on your hand,
your arm, your shoulder.

May I have a moment with Mary?
We didn't know her,
this aide from the night shift,
who had bathed and dressed you
early morning, each day—
now standing in the doorway,
summoning, through obvious shyness,
this intrusion. Her need
to be with you, a regenerative salve
for all we missed, all we could not know,
the years, you here, in the nursing home.
Now this graceful backwash, such a one
as her, with you, caring for you.

              Your breath, less,
and your breath, less   and less   and with ease.
         Surely you willed this, your easy breath.

              We, *of* your breathing,
and of the oil we swabbed onto your lips,
and our bending to you, and the silence
between us,   you,   your breathing—
its ease,   its common   uncommon   mechanical
rhythm   then slowing until a faint
rasp   still slowing   and slowing   and then
no more   no more.

                              Your nurse,
long beloved, this night staying late
into the night—for us—
for this—to come in to you,
and say *it is so*. And to ask us
to leave so she could clean and prepare
your body.

                        Then   finally
with you   the bedcovers precise, drawn
under your arms—your face, your chest,
your arms, your hands
exposed—   a stillness
total and new—
            an absence and a presence—
our needing this time
near your body. You, among us—
unhoused.

Kintsugi Prayer

Let us bow before this art—the broken pieces, the gold-laden
      lacquer, the work of rejoining, the filigreed whole, the bowl
      of repair.

Grant us a history undisguised.

Give us hands to hold what is secured, and eyes unshielded
      from the shine—the broken, fastened.

Let pieces veined white on white name her, the long artery
      of her illness, her distance from us, and from herself.

Hold us again in the *us* before she fell away.

All that was turned away from, all that was upheld—
      these fragments—colorings both orange-rose and shadow,
      and the flesh color the clay at water's edge—
      humble us before such visibility.

Perfect in us what is beyond discernment. As the dark bitter-skinned
      grapes, shattered and shattered until wine, its hue, its taste,
      complete.

The bowl re-composed, steady these hands that take it up.
                                    Will it hold?

Holy Maker, will these seams hold?

Then guide us—some wooden mallet, grasped, and steered in even
      pressure along the bowl's outside rim.   Until the sound.
      The sound.

Let this bowl—let this continuance—sing.   Each strain
      of gold—a wobble, in the round circling sound.

Exalt in us what is re-joined. The whole—seen. Its fastening
heard. Grant us grace.

Grant us grace. All resounding.

Jeannie Gambill was raised in West Texas and Southeast Georgia. The differences between these places—the terrain, the trees, the smells, the culture, the manner of speech, the voices' inflections—have fueled deep wonderment since a child through adulthood, and sparked much of her beginning interest in writing poetry.

Jeannie's graduate work focused on aesthetic development in young children and connections between music literacy and language literacy, especially the effects of traditional songs, rhymes, and singing games on language learning. She has enjoyed fostering musical and artistic abilities in young children, and training teachers in these areas.

With the encouragement of good friend and poet, Vassar Miller, Jeannie's interest in writing grew, and then became a necessity for her when her mother was diagnosed with early onset Alzheimers. Poetry was a path out of the grief and a way to reconnect with and process her world. She heeded Vassar's advice to "get instruction." Because of the vital poetry community in Houston, Jeannie has been privileged to study with Tony Hoagland, Joyce James, Paul Otremba, Kevin Prufer, Robin Reagler, Martha Serpas, and extensively with Sasha West.

Gambill received the Dana Award for Poetry, was a winner in the ART*lines* Ekphrastic Poetry Competition, and a finalist in the Ruth G. Hardman/Nimrod Poetry Competition. She was a featured poet in Houston's Public Poetry Reading Series. Her poetry has appeared in *Cenizo, Gulf Coast, Plainsongs, Voices de la Luna*, and has been anthologized in *The Weight of Addition: An Anthology of Texas Poetry* (Mutabilis Press), *Untameable City: Poems on the Nature of Houston* (Mutabilis Press), and other anthologies.

Jeannie Gambill resides in Bellaire, Texas, but frequents a rustic cabin at the edge of Sam Houston National Forest. She can be reached at jeanniegambill@comcast.net.

CPSIA information can be obtained
at www.ICGtesting.com
Printed in the USA
BVHW040855130223
658403BV00002B/162